THE EIGHT WONDERS OF CHINA

by

**Cheung Wai Kwok,
Koding Kingdom & Ko Sing**

LEARNING HISTORY FROM STORIES

— by Cheung Wai Kwok

As a veteran teacher of a university's history department for over forty years, I am no stranger to these questions – "What's the point of studying history?" "Why do we have to learn about those irrelevant events?" "Studying history is just cramming. So dull and boring!" I disagree, for sure.

Is history irrelevant to us? Certainly not. History, albeit a study of the past, is closely knitted to the present. To those who mock me for telling tales of the dead, I reply, " The Duke of Zhou, Confucius, the Emperor of Qin, Emperor Wu of Han, Li Bai, and Su Shi are no doubt six feet under, but so are Washington, Lincoln, Napoleon, and Gandhi, aren't they? Hong Kong's beloved Yam Kim Fai and James Wong

have already passed away, but their words, their deeds and masterpieces still live vividly in our memories. So, is history really a relic from a bygone age?"

We do not document history for ourselves. History is a collective memory that connects members in the community. Imagine – how can someone without any knowledge of Confucius, Guan Yu, Yue Fei, Man Tin Cheung, the Revolution of 1911 or the Second Sino-Japanese War be identified as a Chinese? Do we respect Zhang Qian (the first envoy to the Western Regions), Zhuge Liang (the dedicated strategist of the Three Kingdoms era) and Judge Bao (the symbol of justice and uprightness) for our own sake? No, the virtues and legacies of these historical figures still live among us and uphold our common values.

We must remember history, every little bit of it. Yet, the fading of history also erases a lot of details. History teachers always want students to memorise as much as possible, like names, locations, years, ranks. Students, on the other hand, find these dry facts irrelevant, meaningless or even annoying. In other words, the way of teaching history suffocates the interest in the subject.

I always think that teachers should breathe life into history, instead of draining it. The paradigm is bound to shift – but how? Storytelling is the most effective way. Students can acquire knowledge of history via stories without, at the very least, feeling repelled. For this reason, I have been collaborating with the Cultural and Education Unit of Radio Television Hong Kong since 1983. Over the last 15 years, I have written eight hundred episodes of Fifty Centuries of China, an audio drama of Chinese history. These eight hundred stories have become food for thought for many audience.

Joint Publishing has the idea to publish a picture book of Chinese history for children. I am pleased to take part in the planning and writing of the book because I believe that history and cultural education can cultivate children's interest. This simple yet enriching picture book is my new and humble attempt to further promote Chinese history.

LEARNING HISTORY VIA MINECRAFT

— **by John Huen**
Founder of Koding Kingdom

In recent years, schools in Sweden, Britain and other countries have been incorporating Minecraft in their curricula. In addition to learning on its own, Minecraft has also been taught with other subjects such as world history – students can reconstruct a historic site and understand the happenings from a first-person perspective, followed by subsequent discussions and drawing of new conclusions. This way of teaching can certainly leave students with a more lasting impression.

Apart from history, Minecraft is also helpful for other subjects. Geography, for instance, can use Minecraft to recreate different geographical contexts to enhance students' understanding.

After all, Minecraft is not only a video game much loved by children, but also a creative, virtual learning platform. Its biggest advantage lies in its ability to engage children easily, nurture team spirit, and build personal leadership. This training of logical thinking is deemed instrumental to their future work and life.

Our team has recreated the Forbidden City in Minecraft lately. The server consists of three levels: the first level plays history animations; the second one involves interactive games; while the last requires users to draw on the history knowledge from the first two levels as well as hints in the Minecraft textbook to answer questions and consolidate their learning. We have shared it with over twenty primary and secondary schools in hopes of facilitating the learning of Chinese history at an early age. So far the reviews have been rather positive that students can find pleasure in learning Chinese history because of Minecraft.

We are very excited to collaborate with various scholars and illustrators to apply the magic of Minecraft on Chinese history. A spark of interest is sufficient enough to fuel children for further learning. They can then take the initiative to research online, look for different angles and descriptions of the historic scenario and, in so doing, enrich their understanding.

Among the eight wonders of China introduced in this book, those with more information available are easier to handle and those with limited references, some of which are inaccurate, require more time. That being said, we do not shy away from these challenges. Buddha statues, for instance, have a lot of sharp points and round corners – which size of grid should we use? Grids that are too big show fewer details; small grids mean a lot of work. Finding the optimal is not an easy task.

To achieve better visual effects, our team has used various textures as well as lights and shades to create different ambiences. We have put a lot of efforts into replicating as much of the real-life sun and sky and waters as possible – hope you will like them!

We sincerely hope that readers will fall in love with Chinese history after reading this book.

CAPTURING THE BEAUTY OF CHINA UP CLOSE

— by Ko Sing

When I was a student, my understanding of China came only from historic events and language classes, such as Lu Xun and the story of butchering an ox, and lacked a more holistic view of what was going on. Taking part in the illustration of The Eight Wonders of China is a very precious opportunity for me.

Never have I realised the beauty of China until it was beheld up-close. The vibrant colours of Tang stand in contrast to another spectrum of hues of the Song and Ming dynasties. I had such an urge to reinterpret the River Scene at Qingming Festival and to take a closer look at the prosperity and urban lives of the Song capital. Unfortunately, it has been done before!

When I was a design and art student,
I studied western art history and knew
almost nothing about Chinese art, which
was such a shame. I used to find Chinese
paintings blurry and monotonous, probably
because of the fading colours. Not until
now can I understand the key to appreciate
Chinese paintings. Chinese paintings require
close examination. Prior knowledge of the
context and meaning enable a completely
different experience. Therefore, I have really
enjoyed the creative process. Rummaging
online for different scenes and information
was an absolute pleasure.

I believe that illustrations of Minecraft style,
as requested by Joint Publishing, can appeal
to teenagers with its liveliness. Over the last
eight years of my design and illustration
career, I have had the fortune to try out
and master a range of styles and topics.
I am very pleased that this project, once
again, proves my potential.

These illustrations took two months of my
spare time and this book fills me with
a sense of satisfaction that is beyond
words and sweeps away the isolation of
working solo. I am looking forward to the
commencement of the next one in the
series, The Eight Wonders of Hong Kong.
Hopefully, I will finally get to meet the
Minecraft team and Professor Cheung.
Such a mysterious working relationship!

CONTENTS

CONTENTS

¹THE PROGRESS OF MATERIAL CIVILISATION

THE PALEOLITHIC AGE (CAVES)

Tens of thousands of years ago, human survived the rough natural conditions by fishing, hunting, and collecting wild fruits. To endure winter's frost and summer's heat and defend against venomous snakes and predators, many resided in natural caves, like Peking Man at Zhoukoudian in Beijing and Lantian Man in Xi'an. They later learnt how to use stones to produce sharp-edged tools and make fire, which marked the beginning of the Paleolithic age.

I   Crafting stone tools

II   Making fire with wood stick

III   Open-fire grilling

IIII   Hunting gear

THE NEOLITHIC AGE (CAVES)

Around ten thousand years ago, human ancestors started to leave their caves and build semi-cave dwellings along the river bank. They made pottery with clay and firing to store food and polished stone tools into more handy equipment. The Neolithic period is, therefore, also known as the New Stone age. Crop farming became the major source of food supplies.

Besides cooking, fire was essential for illumination, scaring predators away, and keeping warm. The livelihood of human ancestors were thus significantly improved.

To construct a semi-cave shelter, people had to dig a pit in the ground before building a roof on it. They could then reside in a more protected environment.

Learning how to make fire was probably the most important invention in human evolution. Inspired by natural wildfire, people gradually acquired the skills of making fire with wood sticks.

TOOLKIT

| 17 Oak Wood | 17:1 Spruce Wood | 5:1 Spruce Wood Plank | 170 Hay Bale | 1 Stone | 4 Cobblestone | 44:3 Cobblestone Slab | 87 Netherrack |

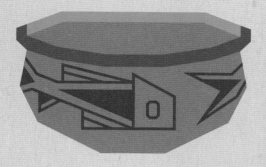

In an enormous country like China, different regions produced potteries of different shapes and patterns. The image features a bowl decorated with a fish with a human face which is discovered at Banpo in Xi'an. The simple embellishment best represented the Yangshao culture of the Central Plain.

During the Neolithic period in China, the most common pottery was li, a three-legged cooking vessel. Li is a hieroglyphic word of a rather smart design. The tripod base allows the container to stand on fire for heating and cooking.

THE NEOLITHIC AGE (SEMI-CAVE)

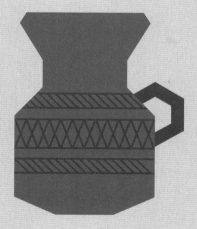

Subsequent conglomeration of regional cultures gave birth to the Longshan culture based in the Central Plain. As a distinctive feature of the culture, the polished black eggshell pottery could withstand fire for a long time. That said, the exquisite and delicate work of art was mostly used for rituals and ceremonies, rather than daily.

Ceramic amphora painted with black and red geometric (usually with swirl or wavy motif) from Gansu was made with local mineral pigments. It signifies the Hongshan culture in northeastern China.

The Five Grains
Rice, wheat, broomcorn, foxtail millet, and maize

The Six Domestic Animals
Horse, ox, sheep, fowl, dog, and pig

THE LATE NEOLITHIC PERIOD
(AGRICULTURE)

What really distinguishes the Neolithic from the Paleolithic era is the escalation from fishing, hunting and collecting wild fruits to animal husbandry and farming. The relatively stable lifestyle allowed the population to grow so tribes started to emerge. All homes were moved up to ground level for better security.

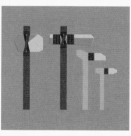

Agricultural equipment of the North

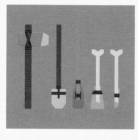

Agricultural equipment of the South

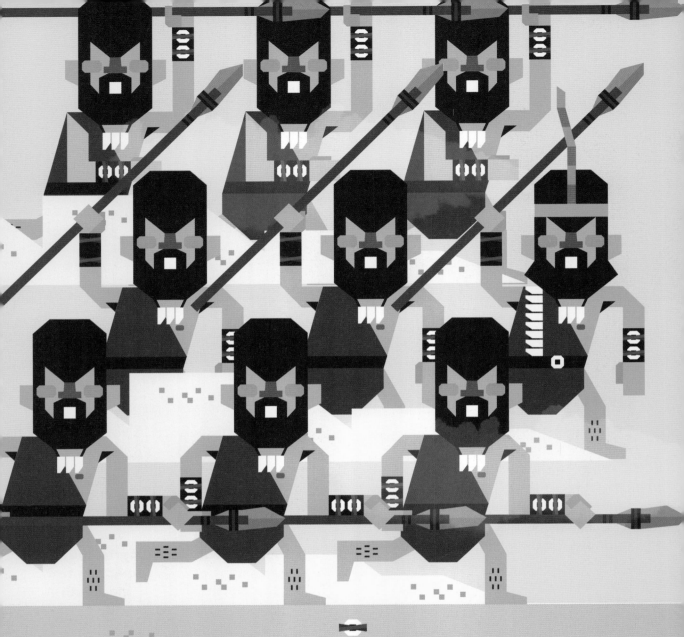

THE BATTLE BETWEEN
THE YELLOW EMPEROR AND CHI YOU

According to ancient Chinese mythology, the legendary Yellow Emperor led various tribes to fight against Chiyou, a bullying tribe leader, in the Late Neolithic Era. The emperor developed the south-pointing chariot to lead his army out of the mist and won a victory against powerful enemies. It is said that culture thrived under his reign. Apart from building large shelters and carts, other inventions credited to the emperor included mathematic calculations, the calendar system, early Chinese astronomy, musical instruments, sericulture, and the first Chinese character writing system. However, almost everything concerning the Yellow Emperor is considered myths and legends.

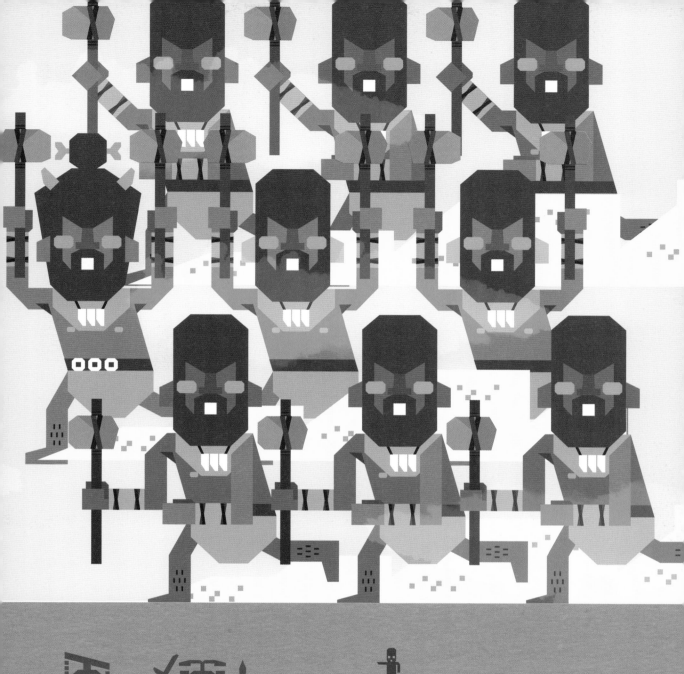

The Yellow Emperor

Chi You

South-pointing chariot

Stone dagger-axe
Stone spear
Stone axe

² THE BIRTH OF MONARCHY

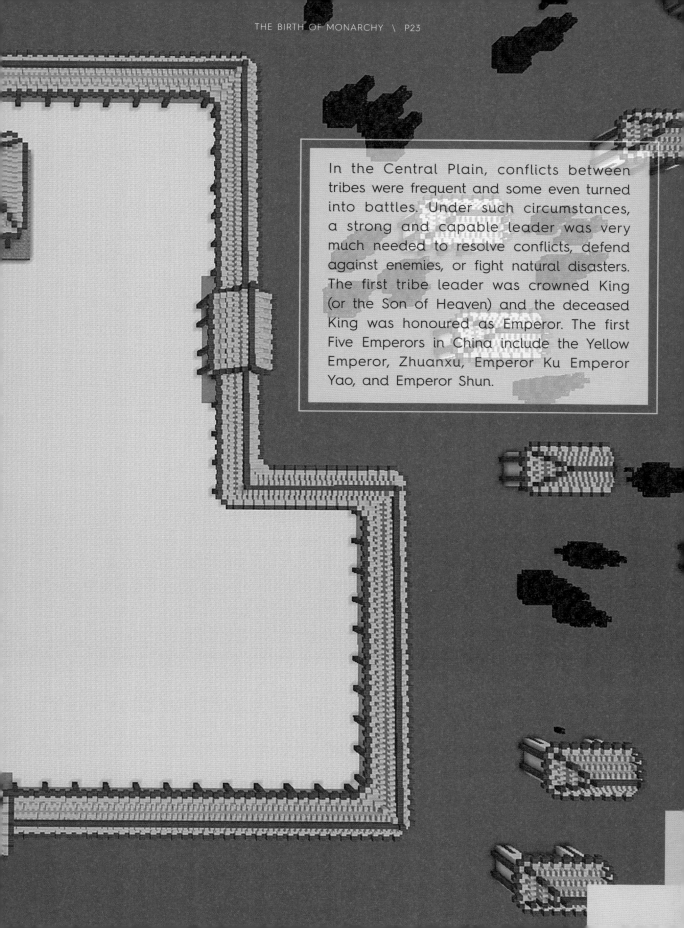

In the Central Plain, conflicts between tribes were frequent and some even turned into battles. Under such circumstances, a strong and capable leader was very much needed to resolve conflicts, defend against enemies, or fight natural disasters. The first tribe leader was crowned King (or the Son of Heaven) and the deceased King was honoured as Emperor. The first Five Emperors in China include the Yellow Emperor, Zhuanxu, Emperor Ku Emperor Yao, and Emperor Shun.

🏛 THE ARCHAEOLOGICAL SITE OF YIN XU

During the reigns of Yao and Shun, the Central Plain was plagued by a great flood.
Yu's success in flood control enabled him the throne. Yu later found the first dynasty in Chinses history, the Xia dynasty, which marked the beginning of a tradition of dynastic succession through primogeniture. The Xia dynasty went into decline few centuries later, whereas the Shang tribe in the east of the Central Plain started to gain momentum. Tang, the chief of the Shang tribe, led people to overthrow Jie, the notorious and alcoholic tyrant of Xia. Tang became king and established the Shang dynasty. Yin Xu (in the present Anyang City in Henan Province) was the capital city of the late Shang Dynasty.

The earliest evidence of the Chinese written language in history was found in Yin Xu. The carefully planned layout of the capital city encircled the Palace and Royal Ancestral Shrines Area with the royal graveyard, houses, pits containing inscribed oracle bones, workshops etc.

TOOLKIT

5:3
Jungle
Wood Plank

5:4
Acacia
Wood Plank

126:4
Acacia
Wood Slab

126:5
Dark Oak
Wood Slab

17
Oak Wood

17:1
Spruce
Wood

The Shang people tended to seek advice from deities or ancestors on critical issues. They carved their queries on turtle plastron or ox scapula, applied intense heat with a hot poker until the bone or shell cracked, and then interpreted the direction of the crack to predict the future. Characters inscribed on the oracle bones are known as the oracle bone script, the earliest known form of Chinese writing. The name of Fu Hao was found inscribed on many of the oracle bones.

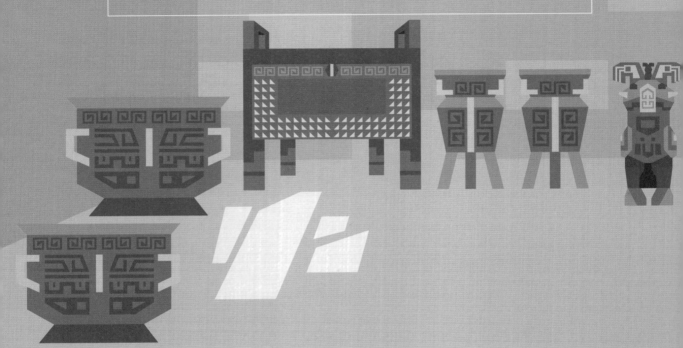

THE TOMB OF FU HAO

Lady Fu Hao, one of the consorts of King Wu Ding of the Shang Dynasty, led numerous military campaigns. The queen-general died at the age of thirty in a battle in the arms of King Wu Ding. A large number of exquisite bronze artefacts – symbols of monarchy and offerings to deities and ancestors – and weapons were unearthed from the Tomb of Fu Hao.

An owl-shaped bronze wine vessel was found at both the Tomb of Fu Hao and the Tomb of King Wu Ding, implying the bonding between the king and the queen.

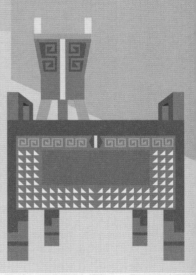

The bronze broad-axe in the tomb is not only a military weapon, but also shows her status and power as a military leader.

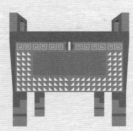

The bronze ding cauldron in the tomb weighs a hundred and forty-seven catties. Three bands of nails running around the rims and the thunder motif on the four legs reveal its use for ritual sacrifices.

The five hundred hairpins in Fu Hao's tomb signify her ladyship.

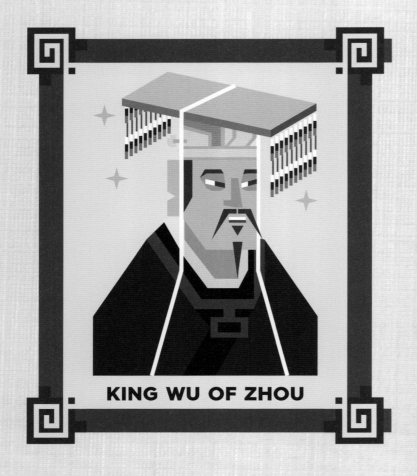

KING WU OF ZHOU

ZHOU

LUOYAN

KING WU OF ZHOU'S REBELLION AND THE FEUDAL SYSTEM

The constant expansion of territory costed the Shang dynasty a weak and exhausted economy. Blinded by arrogance, King Zhou of Shang was keen to kill the patriotic ministers who presented him with good advice. People from all walks of life lost hope in Shang. The Shang dynasty was finally overthrown by Zhou, an agricultural tribe in the west (near the present Xi'an in Shaanxi Province). King Wu of Zhou and his brother Duke Wen of Zhou defeated the Shang dynasty and enfeoffed their fellow warriors and relatives with the strategic lands in the east for better administration of the kingdom.

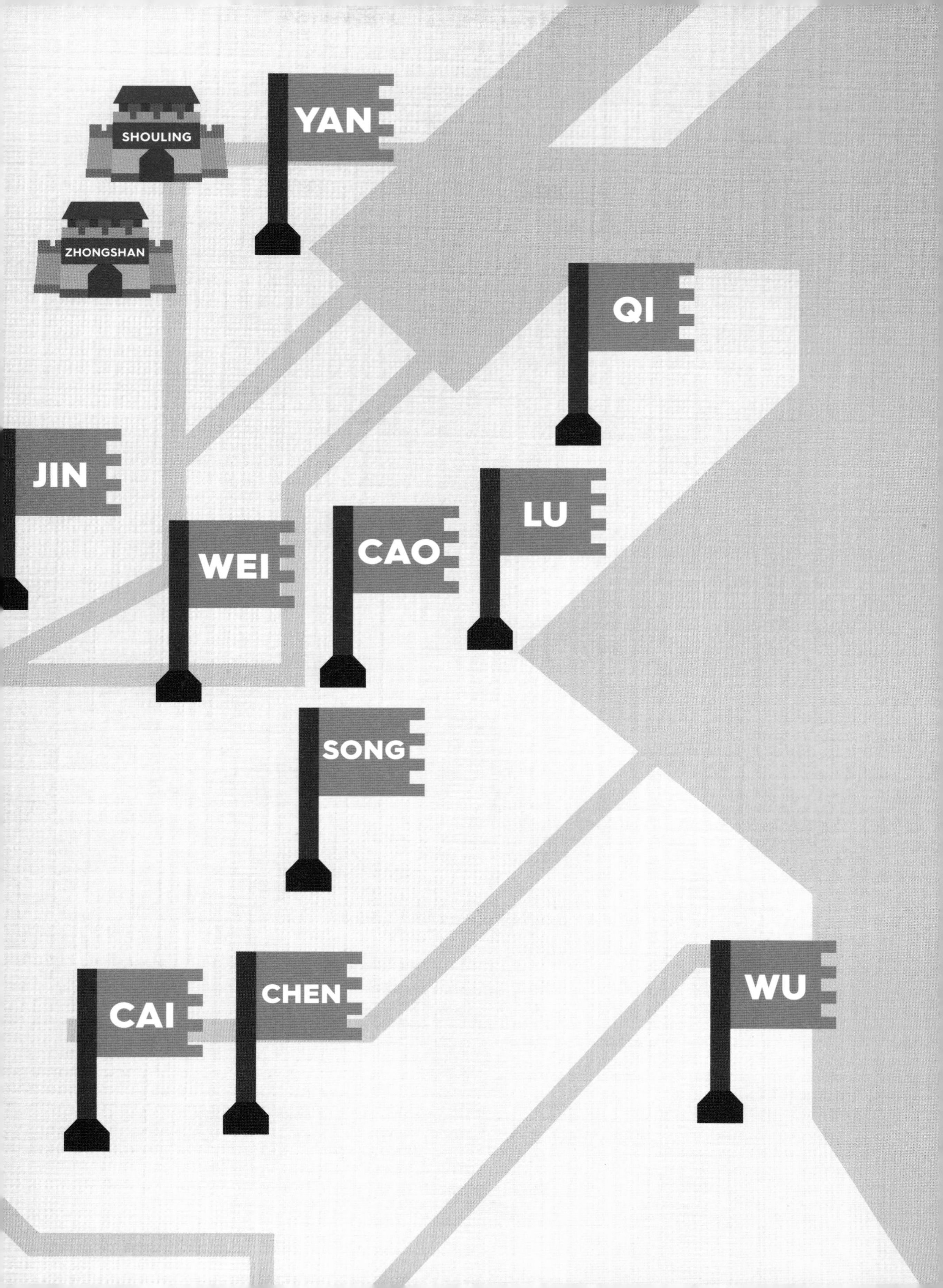
YAN
SHOULING
ZHONGSHAN
QI
JIN
WEI
CAO
LU
SONG
CAI
CHEN
WU

CONFUCIUS TOURING THE KINGDOMS

Confucius was born in the Lu state. Deeply disappointed with Lu's political instability, Confucius resolved to leave Lu with his disciples at the age of thirty and seek better opportunities in other kingdoms. He began a long tour to Wei, Cao, Song, and Chen and attempted to head west to Jin and south to Chu. His enthusiasm to expound his beliefs of benevolent government and virtue politics was met with the blatant disinterest of the courts of these states and hampered navigation caused by wars. Confucius visited over

eighty places during his fourteen-year journey before returning home to his native Lu. He transmitted ancient wisdom and history via a set of texts called the Five Classics. The Five Classics – consisting of the Classic of Poetry, the Book of Documents, the Book of Changes, the Book of Rites, and the Spring and Autumn Annals – has been a staple text for examinations in China throughout millennia.

With over three thousand students, Confucius, the founder of Confucianism, was known for his devotion to teaching. He is remembered as "the greatest sage and teacher" in Chinese history.

I   **The Terracotta Army**

II   **Shang Yang,
the pioneer of
Qin's unification**

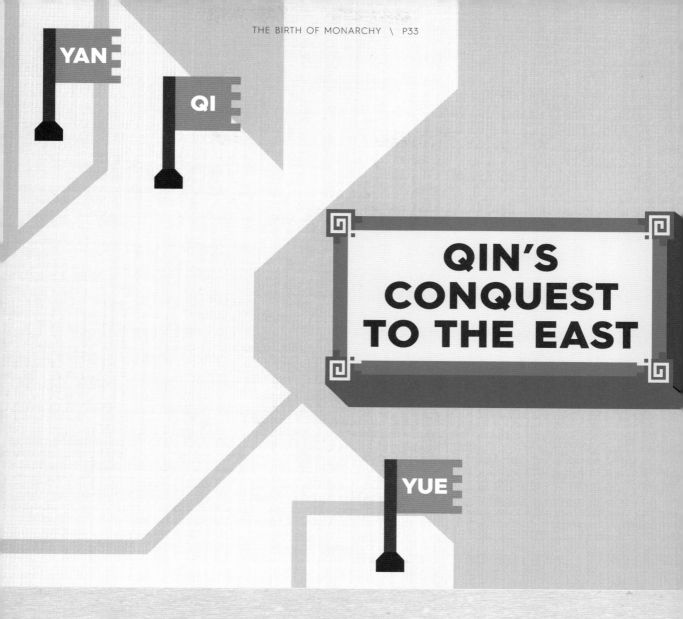

QIN'S CONQUEST TO THE EAST

The King of Zhou was so impressed with the outstanding horse breeding and driving skills of the Qin ancestors that he awarded them a fief on the western border neighbouring the Rong tribes. As the Qin state was obliged to defend against the Rong, the Duke of Qin adopted the conciliation policy through political marriages, until he seized the opportunity to conquer and take over the territories of the tribes. Over the four centuries of twenty generations, Qin was always keen on expanding into the east. Following their strategy of "befriending the distant states while attacking the nearby ones", Qin first conquered Han, Wei, and Zhao in vicinity, before making its way to Chu and finally Yan and Qi. Qin's victory over the six states brought the unification of China.

After the five centuries of conquests and unifications during the Spring and Autumn period and the Warring States period, the number of vassal states dropped significantly from a few hundreds to less than twenty. The major states prioritised the policy of "rich country, strong army" to gain national strength. Such empowerment involved the revision of old systems, the replacement of aristocracy with meritocracy where ordinary citizens could participate in politics, and the drafting of the laws. The entire territory was divided into household units to facilitate tax collection and military recruitment and, in so doing, to enable centralised government control. This history books recorded above as "the reforms".

3 THE UNIFICATION OF QIN AND HAN

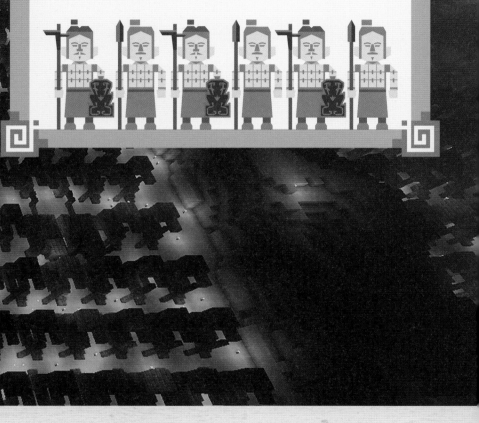

Qin conducted the most successful reforms among the Warring States. Duke Xiao of Qin appointed Shang Yang from Wei as the chief of the reforms – a decision which eventually allowed Qin to rise to prominence. Qin suspended the well-field system and introduced private land ownership where people from different states were welcome to immigrate to Qin to cultivate wastelands. With the help of hydraulic engineers, Qin developed a large-scale irrigation system and constructed canals for more fertile agricultural yield, not to mention the gallant cavalry of Qin. All these contributed to Qin's ultimate success in unification.

TOOLKIT

1
Stone

4
Cobblestone

44
Stone Slab

109
Stone
Brick Stairs

24
Sandstone

24:1
Chiseled
Sandstone

24:2
Smooth
Sandstone

QIN'S MILITARY ADVANCEMENT

Qin was renowned for its highly disciplined army and advanced weaponry. The crossbow had a shooting range of a hundred and fifty metres, which was far more powerful than the composite bow used earlier. They managed to solve the technical issues and enhanced the hardness and durability of bronze weaponry. The combat vehicles and cavalry of Qin disproportionately outweighed that of the other six states. Most importantly, the geographical proximity to the Rong tribes in the west boosted the warfighting capability of Qin's soldiers.

Spear

Crossbow

Bronze
sword

Dagger-axe
and shield

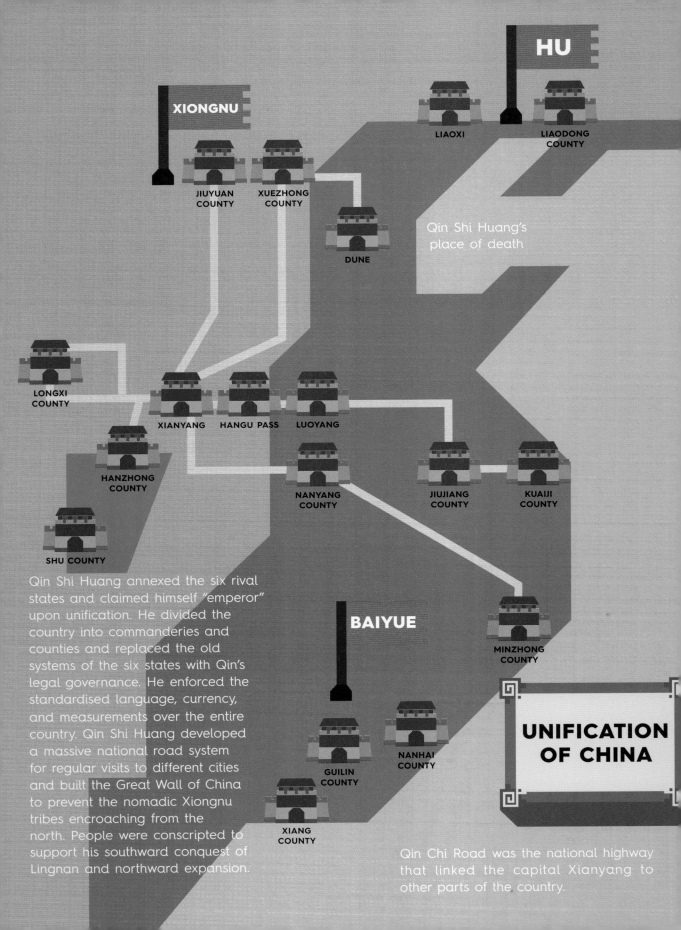

HU

XIONGNU

LIAOXI

LIAODONG
COUNTY

JIUYUAN
COUNTY

XUEZHONG
COUNTY

DUNE

Qin Shi Huang's
place of death

LONGXI
COUNTY

XIANYANG   HANGU PASS   LUOYANG

HANZHONG
COUNTY

NANYANG
COUNTY

JIUJIANG
COUNTY

KUAIJI
COUNTY

SHU COUNTY

Qin Shi Huang annexed the six rival
states and claimed himself "emperor"
upon unification. He divided the
country into commanderies and
counties and replaced the old
systems of the six states with Qin's
legal governance. He enforced the
standardised language, currency,
and measurements over the entire
country. Qin Shi Huang developed
a massive national road system
for regular visits to different cities
and built the Great Wall of China
to prevent the nomadic Xiongnu
tribes encroaching from the
north. People were conscripted to
support his southward conquest of
Lingnan and northward expansion.

BAIYUE

MINZHONG
COUNTY

UNIFICATION
OF CHINA

GUILIN
COUNTY

NANHAI
COUNTY

XIANG
COUNTY

Qin Chi Road was the national highway
that linked the capital Xianyang to
other parts of the country.

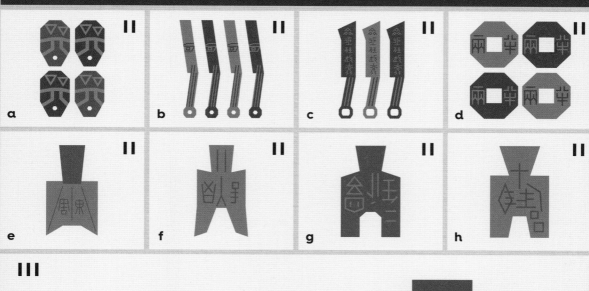

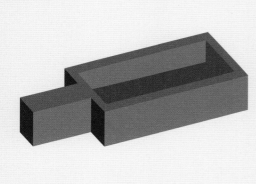

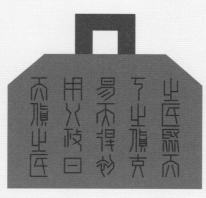

I **Qin's Writing (Small seal script)**

Interpretation
The emperor founded the country
In his glorious dates.
Generations of heirs to succeed.

II **Money of various states**

a   Ant-nose coin of Chu
b   Knife money of Yan
c   Knife money of Qi
d   Half tael of Qin
e   Hollow-handled spade
    of Eastern Zhou
f   Pointed foot spade of Zhao
g   Arched foot spade of Wei
h   Square foot spade of Han

III **Weights and
measures of Qin**

a   Square bronze vessel
    of Qin
b   Weight cast of Qin

THE CHU-HAN CONTENTION

Qin was gripped by power struggle after the death of Qin Shi Huang. Zhao Gao and Li Si conspired to kill Fusu, Qin's eldest son, and made the younger son Huhai the throne as the second emperor of Qin. People of the former six states rebelled against Qin's oppressive conscription and forced labour. Chen Sheng and Wu Guang started the Dazexiang Uprising, which sparked off generals of the six states to revolt in different cities. Xiang Yu from a prominent family in Chu and Liu Bang of peasant origin were the most influential among the rebel leaders. He became the leader of the insurgents after his victory over the Qin generals Zhang Han and Wang Li. Liu Bang led his forces into the Qin capital Xianyang, but did not proclaim himself king. Xiang Yu, on the other hand, made his way to Qin and announced himself the "Hegemon King of Western Chu". Xiang Yu appointed rebel generals as vassal kings and Liu Bang was granted the title "King of Han".

CHU

PENGCHENG

GAIXIA

The former allies were discontent with the unjust enfeoffment that Qi and Zhao waged war against Western Chu. Liu Bang followed suit and unveiled the Chu–Han Contention that lasted for five years. The King of Han rallied regional forces including Qi, Zhao, Liang, Jiujiang and defeated Xiang Yu, hence the establishment of the Han dynasty.

XIANYANG

HAN

HONG GATE

NANZHENG

HAN'S POLITICAL AND MILITARY ACHIEVEMENTS

The early policies of the Han dynasty – for instance, the tax reduction, permission to private minting of coins, and abolition of torturous punishments – not only facilitated the economic and social recovery, but also reinstated confidence in the central government. The meritocratic election system encouraged local officials to recommend virtuous and capable talent among the people and allowed commoners to offer their own services. The government was thus populated by scholars from all walks of life. Military-wise, Xiongnu in the north and Nanyue in the south were deemed the biggest external threats. At first, Han adopted a defence-oriented appeasement approach to maintain peace by paying tribute and forming political marriage to ally with neighbouring nomadic tribes. Emperor Wu, after having ascended the throne, started advocating military campaigns. He invaded the Korean Peninsula in the east, settled Baiyue in the south, repelled the Yi in the southwest, conquered the Qiang in the west, and dispatched his envoy to form an alliance with the Western Regions. Emperor Wu did not only expand the empire's borders significantly, but also spread the reputation of the Han dynasty.

THE WESTERN REGIONS

KUCHA

YUEWEN

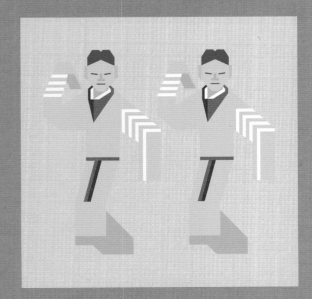

THE GREAT CHIEF'S COMPOUND

DONGHU

THE PROTECTORATE OF THE WESTERN REGIONS

YUMEN PASS

YANG PASS

DUNHUANG

XIONGNU

SHANSHAN

QIANG

THE GREAT WALL

| I | II | III |

I   Elegant Han tomb figures

II   Yellow ochre cloud-riding embroidery

III   Han lacquerware

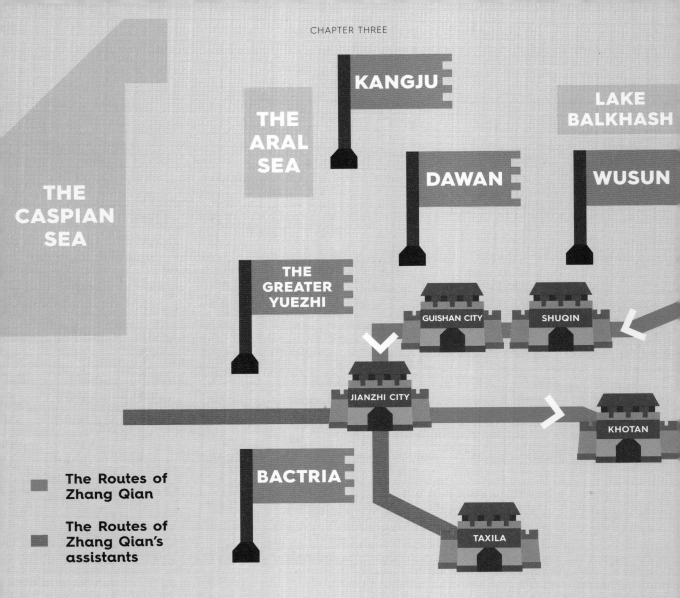

THE CASPIAN SEA

THE ARAL SEA

KANGJU

LAKE BALKHASH

DAWAN

WUSUN

THE GREATER YUEZHI

GUISHAN CITY

SHUQIN

JIANZHI CITY

KHOTAN

The Routes of Zhang Qian

The Routes of Zhang Qian's assistants

BACTRIA

TAXILA

ZHANG QIAN'S DIPLOMATIC MISSIONS TO THE WESTERN REGIONS

Emperor Wu of Han sent Zhang Qian to the Western Regions to form an alliance with the Greater Yuezhi against the Xiongnu. Despite being captured and enslaved by the Xiongnu for ten years, Zhang Qian finally managed to escape and accomplish his mission. He shared intelligence about the Western Regions to Emperor Wu. Since then, the Central Plain started frequent contacts with the Western Regions, which also initiated the cultural exchange between the east and west. Sesame, carrot, wool, traditional Wu attire, Wu music, camel, Ferghana horse and other Central Asian resources were imported to China. At the same time, China also exported a massive amount of silk to the Western Regions, naming the trade route "Silk Road".

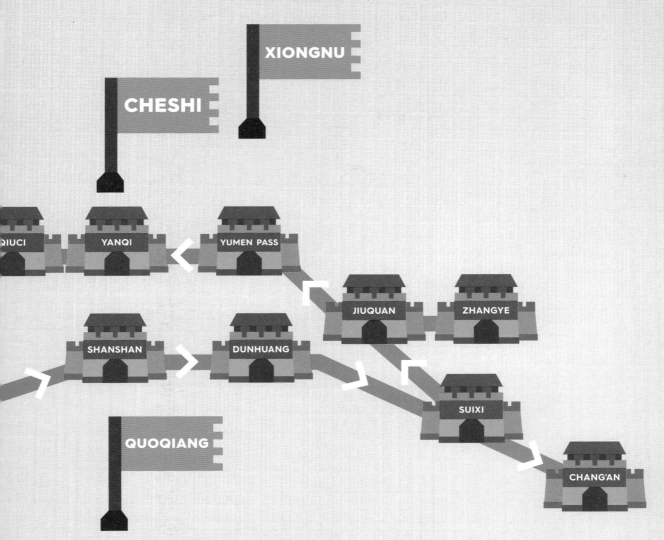

XIONGNU

CHESHI

QIUCI YANQI YUMEN PASS

JIUQUAN ZHANGYE

SHANSHAN DUNHUANG

SUIXI

QUOQIANG

CHANG'AN

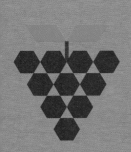

Imported grapes

Imported Ferghana horse

Exported ritual bronzes

Exported Silk

⁴ SPREADING BUDDHISM TO THE EAST

The reign of the Han dynasty lasted for over four hundred years. The later days of the dynasty were plagued by political struggles between eunuchs and empresses' clans. Righteous ministers were ostracised and the corruption of government officials grew to an intolerable level. Regional warlords' ignorance of the law and order accentuated the already appalling wealth gap and hardship of people. Having their hands tied by the harsh reality, people turned to seek emotional refuge and spiritual relief in religion. The two major religions of the Han dynasty were Taoism from the Central Plain, Buddhism from India and the Western Regions.

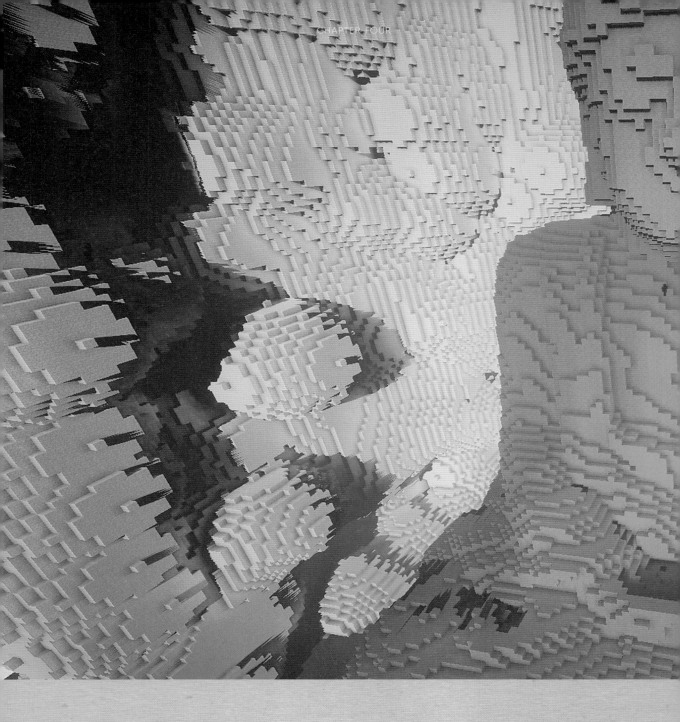

The whole country, which was swept by political turbulence at the end of the Han dynasty, first experienced fierce conflicts between warlords and then the emergence of the Three Kingdoms, followed by the Rebellion of the Eight Kings in the Jin dynasty. The century-long military and political unrest left people in a constant state of despairing uncertainty. Buddhist philosophy highlights the importance of departing from suffering and being at peace with transience and instability. Only through letting go of all attachments can one be liberated from the suffering-laden cycle of existence.

SAKYAMUNI BUDDHA

Buddhism originated in India. Founder Sakyamuni, who was born a prince, deeply empathised with the pain of ageing, sickness, and death in life so he left his power and wealth behind for an ascetic life among commoners. After ceaseless contemplation on how to forego misery, he finally attained enlightenment under a bodhi tree. He identified desire as the root of all sufferings and termination of all desires is the only way to true liberation. The Buddha's teaching was widely circulated in India and subsequently disseminated into the Western Regions. Buddhism was said to have reached the soil of the Central Plain during the reign of Emperor Wu of Han, but it was not propagated until the reign of Emperor Ming of Han. Back in those days, Buddhism was considered a branch of Taoism and was known as Buddha's doctrine.

TOOLKIT

| 179 Red Sandstone | 179:1 Chiseled Red Sandstone | 179:2 Smooth Red Sandstone | 180 Red Sandstone Stairs | 181 Double Red Sandstone Slab | 182 Red Sandstone Slab | 24 Sandstone | 24:1 Chiseled Sandstone | 24.2 Smooth Sandstone |

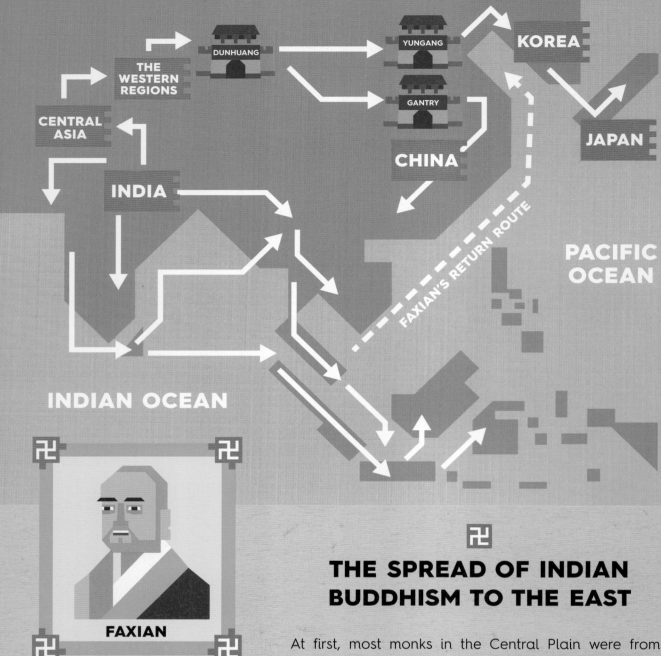

FAXIAN

THE SPREAD OF INDIAN BUDDHISM TO THE EAST

At first, most monks in the Central Plain were from India or the Western Regions and only a few were Han Chinese. Zhu Shixing of the Three Kingdoms, whose Dharma name was Bajie, was the first Han Chinese monk according to the traditional account. He was the model on which Zhu Bajie of the novel Journey to the West was based. Faxian (whose surname was Kung) from Shanxi Province was tonsured at the age of three. At the time of the Sixteen Kingdoms and the Eastern Jin dynasty, Faxian found that the Mahāyāna scriptures were rare and the copies of the Buddhist Disciplines were incomplete. He started his journey from Chang'an to India via the Western Regions at the age of sixty-two and visited thirty countries on the way. Having collected a large amount of Sanskrit Buddhist texts, he took the sea route back to China after fourteen years. Faxian was the first recorded traveller who went to India for the acquisition of Buddhist works. His travelogue A Record of Buddhist Kingdoms had huge influence on Xuanzang, another monk who later visited India for the same purpose.

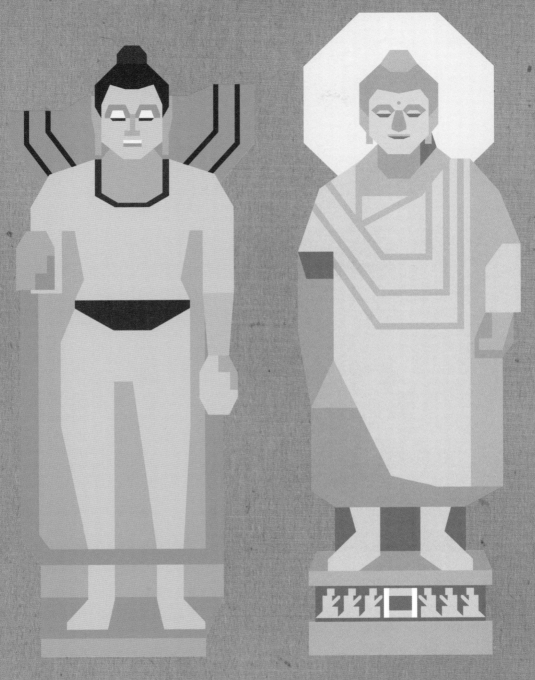

Indian Buddha statues generally have higher nose bridges and deeper eyes - facial features of North Indians. Their plain tight-fitting robes are not only designed to cope with the heat of India, but also reminiscent of the Buddha's simple, ascetic life of sādhanā.

Much influenced by Greek style, the (now dynamited) Buddhas of Bamiyan in Afghanistan displayed more realistic accurate details of human anatomy.

Murals in Dunhuang (The Western Wei period)

Early Buddha statues in Dunhuang (The Northern Liang in the Sixteen Kingdoms)

THE MOGAO CAVES IN DUNHUANG

When Buddhism made its way from the Western Regions to the Central Plain, monks first reached Dunhuang, the west entrance of the Hexi Corridor, and waited for the opportunity to reach their destination. During the Former Qin period of the Sixteen Kingdoms, Le Zun, a notable Buddhist monk, started to excavate caves for sādhanā at Mount Sanwei in Dunhuang, which were later known as the Mogao Caves. More and more caves were constructed throughout the few centuries of the Northern Wei, Northern Zhou, Sui, Tang, and the Five Dynasties. These caves were home to a wealth of treasures – stone Buddha statues, murals, clay sculptures, Buddhist manuscripts and texts of the Tang and Song dynasties. Most of them are now housed in foreign museums. The Dunhuang Caves is not only treasure troves of ancient Chinese Buddhist art, but is also listed as one of the UNESCO World Heritage Sites.

The sculptures built during the heyday of the Tang dynasty have fuller faces and show more Han Chinese elements. With more balanced body ratio and less exposed clothing, they no longer have the disproportionately huge heads and stiff postures like the old Buddha statues do.

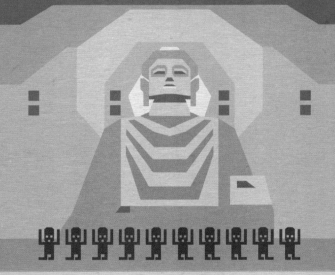

NORTHERN BUDDHIST STATUES

During the Sixteen Kingdoms, many of the Hu leaders who emigrated to the Central Plain were believers of Buddhism and facilitated the growing popularity of Buddhism in northern China. The Tuoba clan of the Xianbei, which unified northern China and established the Northern Wei dynasty, also favoured Buddhism and excavated the Yungang Grottoes (top image) – a majestic Buddhist sculptural site near the capital Pingcheng (now Datong City in the province of Shanxi). Emperor Xiaowen of Northern Wei moved the capital to Luoyang and subsequently constructed the massive Longmen Grottoes (bottom image) in the new capital's countryside.

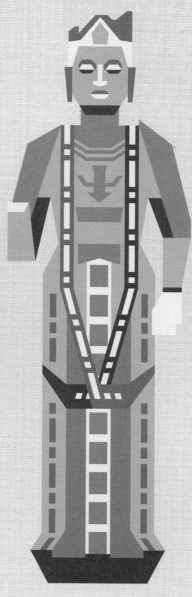

The Yungang Grottoes has preserved more Buddha sculptures of old Indian and Greek style – the former wears thinner, elegant clothes and the latter has thicker garments. The Longmen Grottoes, which was built later, features more sinicized style and subjects. The above image shows a statue at the Yungang Grottoes and statue that is carved later (bottom image on the right) displays more local features.

The gilded and painted stone sculpture of Bodhisattva of the Northern Qi dynasty wears thin tight-fitting clothes with accessories. The simplistic carving skills delineate a dimensional, well-built physique. It is an important piece that marks from the transitional period from the Northern Wei to the Sui and Tang dynasties.

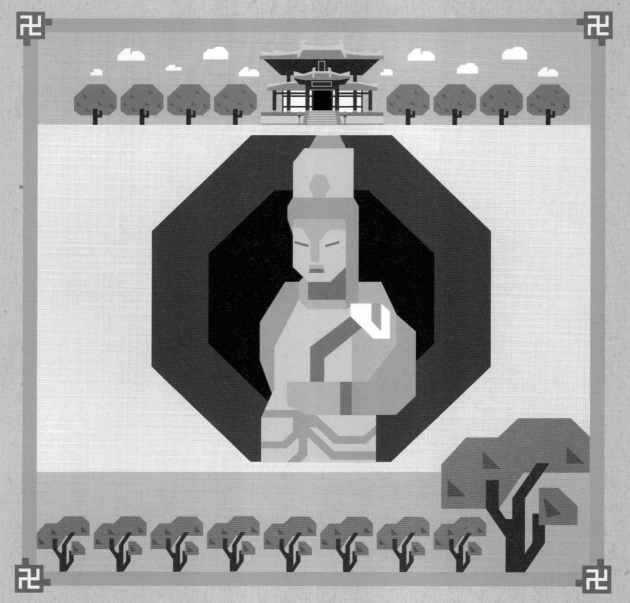

SOUTHERN BUDDHIST STATUES

The ongoing civil war between the Wei and Jin dynasties led to the invasion of the Five Barbarians. Many Chinese aristocrats and scholars, most of who were deeply influenced by Taoism, fled to the Huai River and the Yangtze Region in the south and founded the Southern (Song, Qi, Liang, Chen) dynasties. During the Qi and Liang dynasties, more royalty and scholars turned to embrace Buddhism. Emperor Wu of Liang built many Buddhist temples and, because of that, Buddhism were in full flourish in the south. Many Buddhist temples of that period can still be found in forests and the architectural style demonstrates explicit Taoist influence and Han cultural features. The stone sculpture of the Qixia Temple shown in the image spells grace and refinement.

Zen became popular in the south of Jiangnan, especially around the Two Hus, the Two Jiangs, Guangdong, and Fujian. Bodhidharma, the founder of Zen Buddhism, travelled to China to proliferate Buddhism and explained precepts to Emperor Wu of Liang during the Northern and Southern dynasties. Because Zen preferred enlightening through truthful conversations, rather than written accounts, most temples in the south have left very few Buddha statues. The mural shown above features a stone sculpture of Temple of Thanksgiving floating on Suzhou Creek. The fact that people worshiped on their knees immediately upon noticing the sculpture implied the general acceptance of Buddhism in Jiangnan. The left image shows a gilt Bodhisattva statue of the Eastern Jin dynasty.

⁵ A DAY IN CHANG'AN

Chang'an of the Tang dynasty was the largest capital in the world. Its surface area was triple of that of Chang'an of the Han dynasty and one and half as large of that of Beijing city during the Ming and Qing dynasties. The populous capital had five hundred thousand households, consisting of royalty, aristocrats, officials, merchants, soldiers, monks and Taoists, craftsmen, foreign emissaries, scholars for further studies or examinations, and civil officials awaiting to attend court.

Chang'an was formed in a rectangular shape and was laid out on a north-south axis in a grid pattern. It was divided into the Palace City (royal residence), Imperial City (government offices), and residential and business districts, with

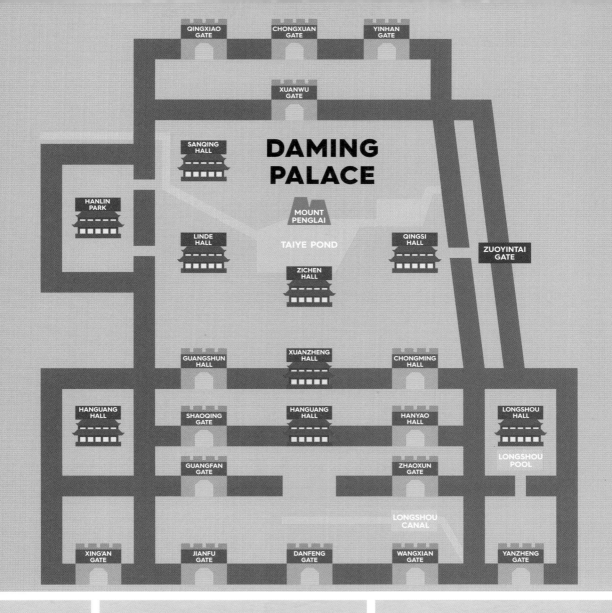

DAMING PALACE

QINGXIAO GATE

CHONGXUAN GATE

YINHAN GATE

XUANWU GATE

SANQING HALL

HANLIN PARK

MOUNT PENGLAI

TAIYE POND

LINDE HALL

QINGSI HALL

ZUOYINTAI GATE

ZICHEN HALL

GUANGSHUN HALL

XUANZHENG HALL

CHONGMING HALL

HANGUANG HALL

SHAOQING GATE

HANGUANG HALL

HANYAO HALL

LONGSHOU HALL

GUANGFAN GATE

ZHAOXUN GATE

LONGSHOU POOL

LONGSHOU CANAL

XING'AN GATE

JIANFU GATE

DANFENG GATE

WANGXIAN GATE

YANZHENG GATE

Hall

government offices

Pond

emperor and his
by numerous gardens

Zichen Hall

The emperor's office and the
north of the hall is the harem

Qingsi Hall

For the emperor's leisure
and entertainment

Hanguang Hall

For imperial obeisance and polo

Longshou Hall

For shows, horse riding,
and entertainment

A DAY OF AN OFFICIAL

When the cock crowed at the break of dawn, officials who were Rank Five or above started to make their way to the hall for morning assembly and waited outside until they were summoned by the emperor. Civil and military officials of Rank Nine or above in the capital only needed to attend the assembly on every first and fifteenth day of the month. There were usually a few hundred to a thousand officials participating in the morning assembly. When the assembly was over, they could enjoy a meal in the Imperial City before returning to their own offices. They finished work in the afternoon and returned home for dinner or to meet with friends. Many famous scholars and writers of the Tang dynasty lived in Chang'an and had the capital mentioned in their poems, stories and literature. For instance, Li Bai, Du Fu, Wang Wei, Han Yu, Liu Zongyuan, Liu Yuxi, and Bai Juyi all resided in Chang'an.

As Du Fu describes the delightful spring gala of female aristocrats in Qujiang in one of his poems, "In the refreshing weather on the third of March, numerous elegant ladies had a fine moment by the riverside of Chang'an City."

A DAY AT THE WEST MARKET

The East Market and the West Market in Chang'an opened at noon and closed at sunset every day. Two east-west and two north-south streets divided the West Market into 9 different city blocks. Each block was cramped with shops that sold clothes, silks, medicines, and iron. Majority of the shops were bistros and restaurants and Huji Tavern was the most renowned among all. Due to its geographical proximity to the starting point of the Silk Road, the West Market gathered a lot of Hu merchants and products including jewelleries and incenses from the Western Regions as well as silks and porcelains from China. The swirling dance performed by Hu girls also attracted a large crowd in the West Market. The market was closed at night because of the curfew. People could only hang up lanterns and celebrate to their hearts' content when the curfew was lifted on the Lantern Festival or national holidays.

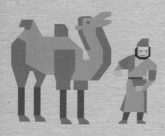

Hu merchants trading in the West Market

White glaze stirrup-shaped pot

Silver tall cup with hunting and plant motifs

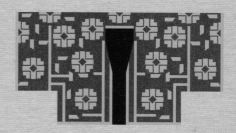

Tang silk golden maiden short-sleeve woven shirt

DA CI'EN TEMPLE

Xuanzang translating Buddhist texts

Among the one hundred and ten wards in Chang'an, there were many well-known Buddhist monasteries and Taoist abbeys. For instance, the Da Ci'en Temple in Jinchang Ward in the south of the city was built by Emperor Taizong of Tang's head prince Li Zhi (later known as Emperor Gaozong of Tang, husband of Wu Zetian) in memory of his mother Empress Zhangsun. The temple was initially known as Jianfu Temple and was one of the three major Buddhist text translation sites. Upon his return to China, Buddhist monk Xuanzang was invited to translate the texts he collected in India at the Da Ci'en Temple. Having stood through millennia of wear and tear, the Giant Wild Goose Pagoda at the back of the temple remains a colossal landmark of Chang'an.

Small Wild Goose Pagoda

When the results of the imperial examination were announced, graduates who passed the court exam could carve their autographs on a stone slab in the Da Ci'en Temple.

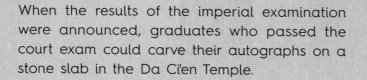

Giant Wild Goose Pagoda

ANNOUNCEMENT

Wild Goose Pagoda Autograph

6 RIVER SCENE AT QINGMING FESTIVAL

After the An Lushan Rebellion against the Tang dynasty, the north of the Central Plain was plagued by struggles among warlords. The largely weakened central government could only rely on the wealth and resources of the southern Central Plain. The Grand Canal thus became the engine of the country's economy. Hangzhou, Suzhou, Bianzhou and other big cities along the Grand Canal were curial to the Caoyun System (the transportation system on the Grand Canal).

As the last stop of the Caoyun System in the Central Plain, Bianzhou was a thriving hub for food and resources and attracted many merchants from different places. It gradually became far more prosperous than Chang'an and the Eastern capital Luoyang in late Tang. The Five Dynasties therefore chose Bianzhou over Chang'an or Luoyang as the capital and renamed it into "the Eastern Capital Kaifeng Fu". The Song dynasty also made Bianzhou its capital after overthrowing the Five Dynasties.

Many of the luxurious goods being transported to Kaifeng were rare treasures from overseas. Merchants from Yi (now Arabia), Persia (now Iran), and the East and West Seas (now Southeast Asian countries) came via the sea route first arrived at ports including Guangzhou and Quanzhou before heading up north via the Grand Canal. They made huge profits by selling jewelleries, incenses, dried seafood and other products in Kaifeng. Song merchants also brought silks, porcelains, and copper coins and set sail to foreign countries as far as Kenya and Tanzania on the East African coast for trading. Wrecks of the Song dynasty can still be found around the coast of Guangdong and Fujian today. The Nanhai One, for instance, was discovered in Yangjiang City in Guangdong Province.

TOOLKIT

5
Oak Wood
Plank

5:1
Spruce
Wood Plank

43:2
Double
Wooden Slab

44:2
Wooden
Slab

53
Oak Wood
Stairs

85
Oak Fence

17
Oak Wood

17:1
Spruce
Wood

A BUSTLING HUB OF SHOPS

The Tang capital was divided into "wards" and "lanes". All the wards within the city were walled and shops were prohibited from the streets. People could only buy household goods on lanes in the wards. Bulk trading was only allowed in the East and West Market within regulated periods. In other words, business activities were much restricted by the central government. During the Five Dynasties, the walls of wards were finally torn down. Shops were lined on the streets and the curfew was lifted. Kaifeng, one of the wealthiest cities back in those days, boasted a thriving commercial hub as well as a population of over one million.

HERBAL MEDICINE

BOOKSHOP

ANCIENT AND MODERN
PROSE AND POETRY

RICE AND GRAIN

THE RISE OF CRAFTS

Craftsmen began to work full-time during the Song dynasty and their works were not only popular within the country, but were also exported to other parts of the world. For instance, the quantity and quality of Song silks, known for how delicate and thin they were, significantly surpassed that of the Tang dynasty. Among the Five Great Kilns emerged in Tang, imperial kiln was known for its subtle yet elegant cracked ice motif. Dark-glazed Jian tea bowl was also a rare gem. The proliferation of woodblock printing enabled the wide circulation of texts including classics, poetry, and history books. The invention of movable type printing press technology was crucial to the dissemination of knowledge and popularisation of academic research.

染坊

Song brocade

Dark-glazed Jian bowl

Cracked ice motif porcelain

URBAN MANAGEMENT

During the Song dynasty, the constant growth of population and the high density of wooden houses and shops exposed Kaifeng to the risks of fire hazard. Under these circumstances, the government introduced some of the world's first fire safety measures. Stricter blackouts, night patrols and outposts in towers were enforced for fire prevention and rescue.

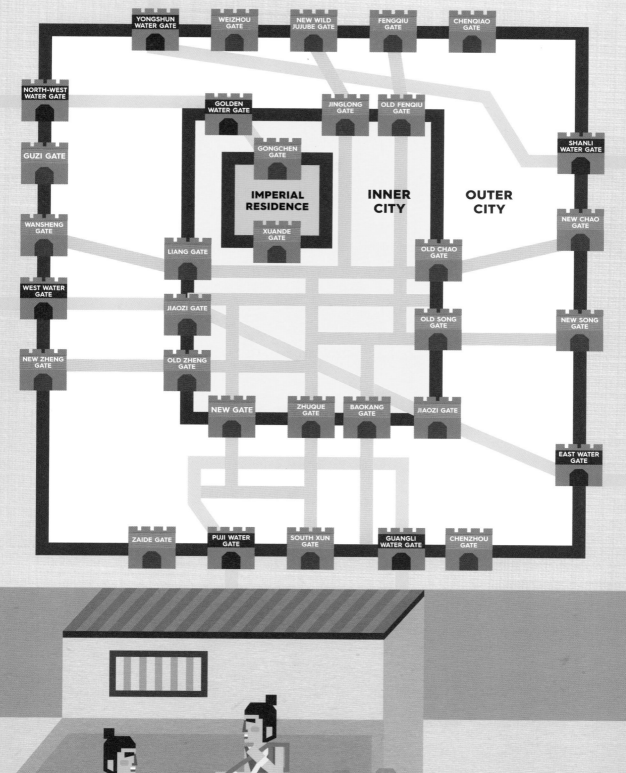

YONGSHUN WATER GATE

WEIZHOU GATE

NEW WILD JUJUBE GATE

FENGQIU GATE

CHENQIAO GATE

NORTH-WEST WATER GATE

GOLDEN WATER GATE

JINGLONG GATE

OLD FENQIU GATE

SHANLI WATER GATE

GUZI GATE

GONGCHEN GATE

IMPERIAL RESIDENCE

INNER CITY

OUTER CITY

WANSHENG GATE

XUANDE GATE

NEW CHAO GATE

LIANG GATE

OLD CHAO GATE

WEST WATER GATE

JIAOZI GATE

OLD SONG GATE

NEW SONG GATE

NEW ZHENG GATE

OLD ZHENG GATE

NEW GATE

ZHUQUE GATE

BAOKANG GATE

JIAOZI GATE

EAST WATER GATE

ZAIDE GATE

PUJI WATER GATE

SOUTH XUN GATE

GUANGLI WATER GATE

CHENZHOU GATE

The numerous canals in Kaifeng were instrumental to the water supply and sewage, enabling better livelihood for city dwellers.

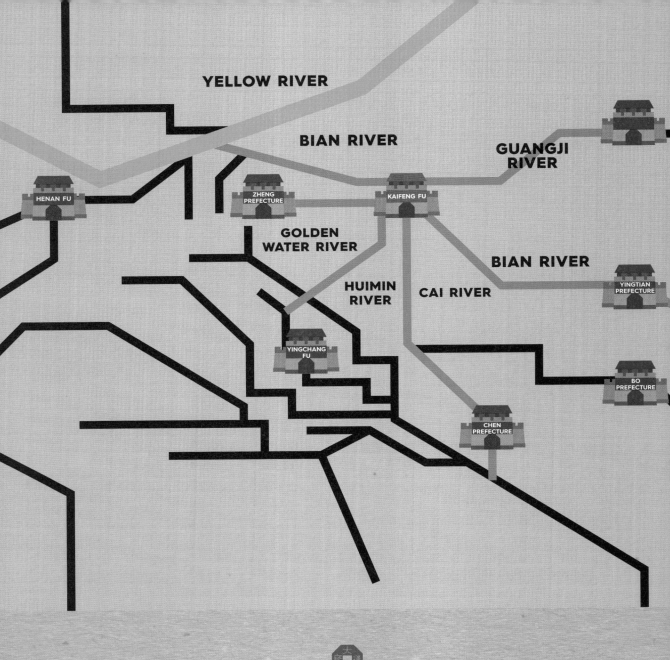

CURRENCY

The notable growth in commercial contacts during the Song dynasty led to significant increase in the volume of business transactions. Since carrying strings and strings of coins around were no longer practical, jiaozi – the first paper money the world has ever seen – was introduced. The government took over the trading receipts circulated among people and officially issued money in paper form. In mid Ming dynasty, damingbaochao (paper note circulated in the Ming dynasty) underwent major depreciation because of excessive issuing and was therefore replaced by foreign silver.

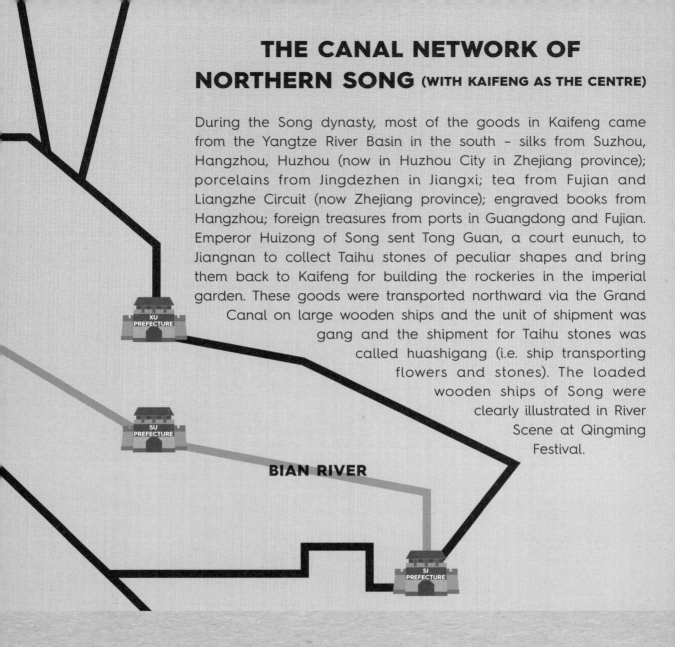

THE CANAL NETWORK OF NORTHERN SONG (WITH KAIFENG AS THE CENTRE)

During the Song dynasty, most of the goods in Kaifeng came from the Yangtze River Basin in the south – silks from Suzhou, Hangzhou, Huzhou (now in Huzhou City in Zhejiang province); porcelains from Jingdezhen in Jiangxi; tea from Fujian and Liangzhe Circuit (now Zhejiang province); engraved books from Hangzhou; foreign treasures from ports in Guangdong and Fujian. Emperor Huizong of Song sent Tong Guan, a court eunuch, to Jiangnan to collect Taihu stones of peculiar shapes and bring them back to Kaifeng for building the rockeries in the imperial garden. These goods were transported northward via the Grand Canal on large wooden ships and the unit of shipment was gang and the shipment for Taihu stones was called huashigang (i.e. ship transporting flowers and stones). The loaded wooden ships of Song were clearly illustrated in River Scene at Qingming Festival.

XU PREFECTURE

SU PREFECTURE

BIAN RIVER

SI PREFECTURE

STERLING SILVER DECANTER EXCHANGE

ALL GOLD AND SILVER ACCESSSORIES

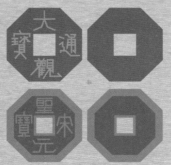

Bureau de Change

Copper Coins (top) Iron coins (bottom)

Unofficial paper money

Government-issued paper money

[7] THE LIFE OF AN INTELLECTUAL

Chu Yuan-Chang, the Hongwu Emperor, rose rapidly in one of the local rebellions against the Yuan dynasty. After years of tough battles, Chu disbanded other rebel groups in the south, drove away the Mongols and founded the Ming dynasty. He made Yingtian (now Nanjing in Jiangsu) the dynastic capital and his son the Yongle Emperor relocated the capital to Beijing while keeping Yingtian as the southern capital, hence the Nanjing-Beijing duo capital system.

Following the unification of China, the Hongwu Emperor swiftly removed the warriors from power and put civil officials forward for important positions. The civil service imperial examinations were enforced to select state officials. The rigorous examination system dominated lives of million literati (intellectuals) throughout the two centuries of the Ming dynasty. The cultural life of Ming also grew in line with the imperial examinations.

The Hongwu Emperor set up schools in various prefectures, subprefectures, and counties and a Confucian temple was built next to every school. The relics of the Ming schools and Confucian temple can still be found in the old towns of many cities.

All students had to pass the county exams to become an entry-level examinee tongsheng. Every prefecture (administrative district of several to more than ten counties) organised an annual county exam for tongsheng of its subsidiary counties. Those who had passed the exam were called shengyuan, also commonly known as xiucai, the lowest ranking in the civil service examination system.

All shengyuan were welcome to participate in the triennial provincial exam held in the provincial capital.

Those who passed the exam were called juren, the first qualification to be an official, and the juren who ranked first in the exam won the title of jieyuan.
The metropolitan exam was held by the Ministry of Rites in the spring following the provincial exam. Jurens from different provinces travelled to the capital city, which was also known as the "journey to the Spring Exam". Those who passed the triennial national exam were entitled gongshi and the gongshi who ranked first was called huiyuan.

TOOLKIT

5
Oak
Wood
Plank

5:1
Spruce
Wood
Plank

5:2
Birch
Wood
Plank

5:3
Jungle
Wood
Plank

5:4
Acacia
Wood
Plank

5:5
Dark Oak
Wood
Plank

17
Oak
Wood

17:1
Spruce
Wood

416
Armor
Stand

321
Painting

MEETING THE EMPEROR IN THE PALACE

Supervised by the emperor himself, the palace exam was held at the Hall of Supreme Harmony in the autumn following the Metropolitan exam, sometime around the Mid-Autumn Festival. All gongshi could attend the palace exam. The exam aimed at ranking candidates in order so no one was subjected to elimination. Graduates were ranked in three classes. Only the top three graduates could get into the first class – zhuangyuan was the first nationwide; bangyan came second overall just below zhuangyuan; tanhua ranked third overall. Candidates in the second class, usually a few dozens of them, were called jinshi chushen. Tong jinshi chushen were the two to three hundred graduates who ranked third class in the palace exam. All graduates in the three classes were called jinshi.

Achieving jinshi meant unlocking a career in the government. Top graduates were recruited in the Hanlin Academy (a research and academic institution where members could gain access to imperial manuscripts and classics) as Xiuzhuan,

Bianxiu, and Shujishi. After their terms in the academy were completed, they would be allocated to different ministries and provinces as mid-ranking officials. Graduates with less outstanding results either served as apprentices in different ministries or as provincial magistrates. Whether the career was a bumpy ride or a smooth sailing was entirely a matter of individual capability and luck.

RANK BADGES

I	Civil official of the 1st rank Crane badge
II	Civil official of the 2nd rank Golden pheasant badge
III	Civil official of the 3rd rank Peacock badge
IIII	Civil official of the 4th rank Anser badge
✛✛✛	Civil official of the 5th rank Silver pheasant badge
✛✛✛✛	Civil official of the 6th rank Egret badge
✛✛✛	Civil official of the 7th Mandarin duck rank badge
✛✛✛	Civil official of the 8th rank Quail badge
✛✛✛✛	Civil official of the 9th rank Paradise flycatcher badge

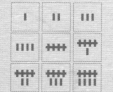

THE AESTHETICS OF LIFE

The cultural life of literati has significantly shaped the Ming society. Calligraphy, painting, gardening, interior decoration, music, and opera were all developed in accordance with the taste of literati. The balance between subtlety and elegance, leisure and composure were designed to reach the ideal aspirations of traditional Chinese cultural community.

Literati also picked household goods that were exemplary of their aesthetics. The Ming furniture was known to the world for its superb choice of materials, meticulous production, and sleek design. The iconic Jingdezhen blue and white

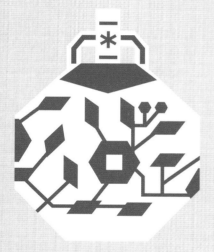

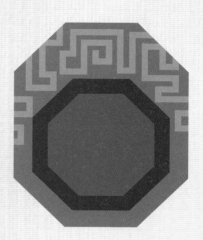

porcelain, made possible with the advancement in technology, entered the scene that was once dominated by monochromatic porcelain. The zoological and botanical motifs, ranging from flowers, birds, bugs, fish, mountains and waters, displayed simplicity, elegance, freedom and passion.

I	II
III	IIII

I   Yoke-back armchair

II   Classic decoration

III Celadon

IIII Ink stone

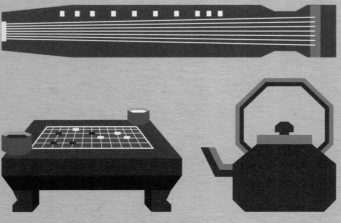

I   Guqin

II   Go

III   Yixing clay teapot

LITERARY GATHERING

In their leisure time, scholars enjoyed meeting up for poetry, tea brewing, art appreciation, music jamming, and chess playing. Their prose and verse, which composed a big part of their cultivation and character, extolled the virtues of harmony. Their landscape and portrait paintings expressed their inner spirit and effortless creativity. Their paintings, most of which were for their own amusement, were significantly different from those of imperial and common artists.

RETREAT TO NATURE

Those who excelled in the civil service examination not only brought honour to their families, but were also highly respected in their hometowns. They returned home for peaceful seclusion in their private gardens upon their retirement. Private gardens were popular in the Ming dynasty. Chinese gardens were usually decorated and designed with small rock mountains and streams, which were always featured in poetry and literature. These gardens, regardless of the size, were designed to create a new idealized scene of nature at every turn. The terraces and pavilions blended seamlessly with the botanic elements. The stone engraved windows on the long, meandering corridors added intriguing frames to the whole experience. The flowers, trees, and artificial mountains changed continually with the four seasons, bringing inexhaustible charms to the garden.

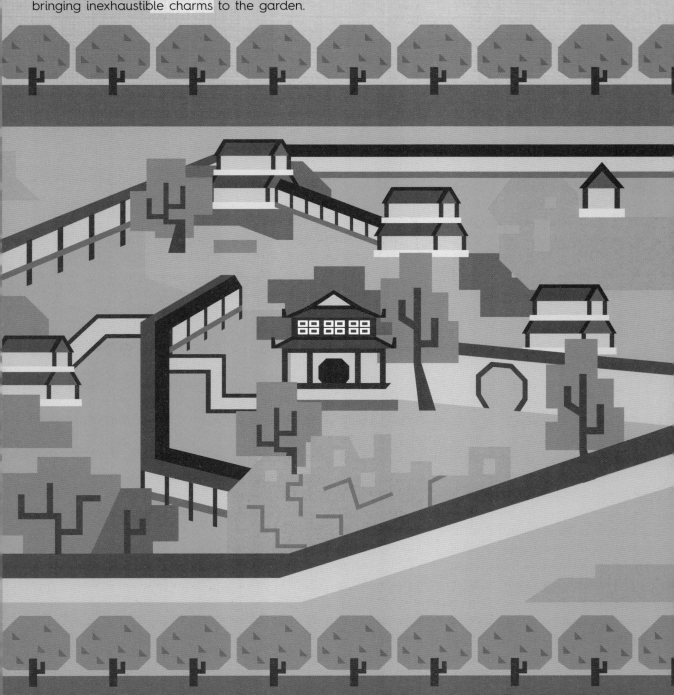

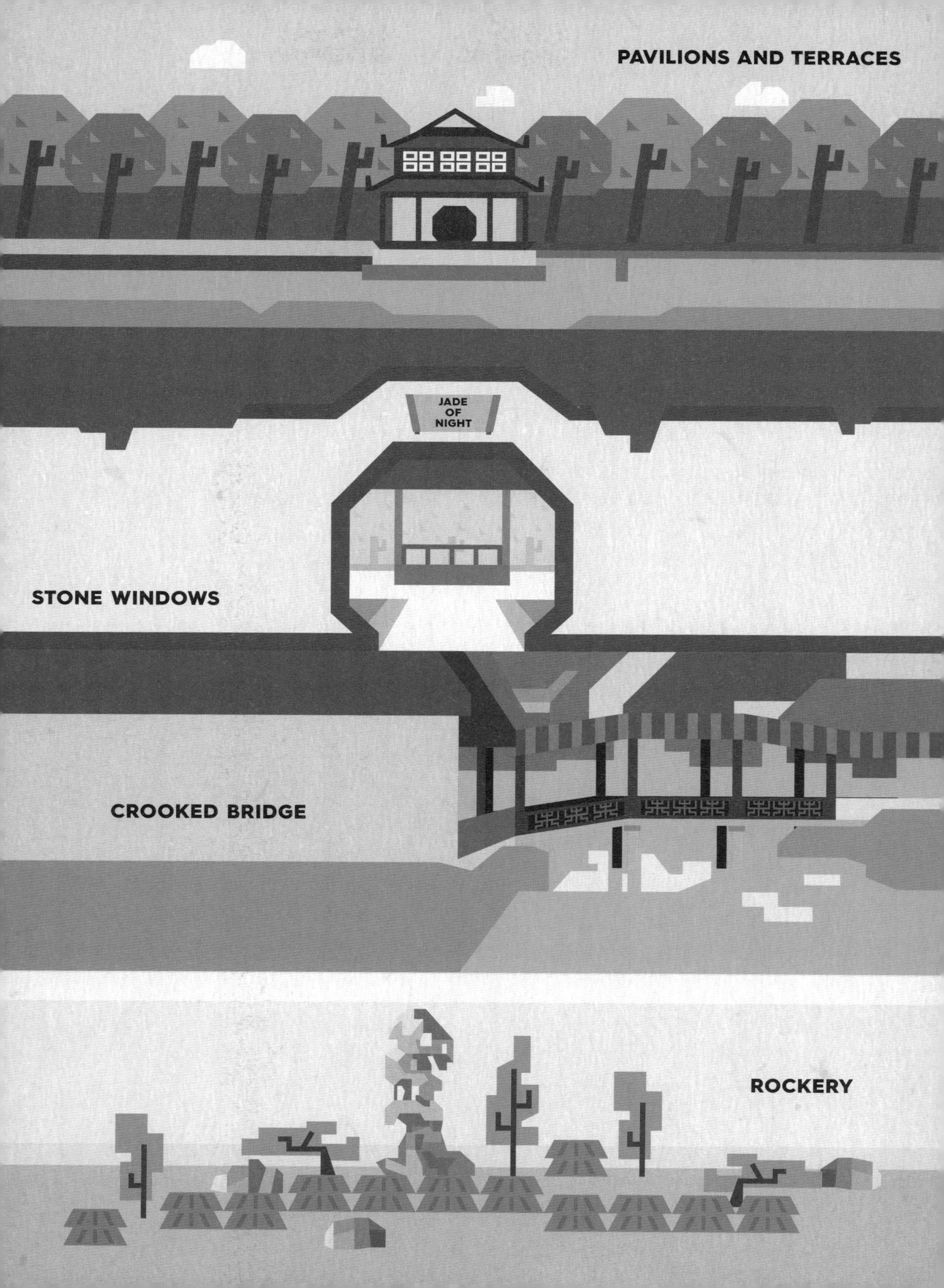

PAVILIONS AND TERRACES

JADE
OF
NIGHT

STONE WINDOWS

CROOKED BRIDGE

ROCKERY

[8]INTEGRATION BETWEEN THE MANCHUS AND HAN CHINESE

The Qing dynasty, with its roots around Mount Baekdu and the Songhua River, was founded by Nurhaci (whose temple name was Taizu) of the House of Aisin Gioro of the Jianzhou Jurchens. The Gioro clan was subordinate to the Ming dynasty at first. After Nurhaci's father and grandfather were killed in an expedition for the Ming army, the Ming reign apologised and offered to compensate Nurhaci with a dukedom. During the mid-Ming period, Japan invaded Korea and the Ming army was sent to aid the Koreans. As the seven years of war left the Liaodong Peninsula undefended, Nurhaci seized the chance to attack neighbouring tribes, unified the Jurchen clan and established the Eight Banners system.

In the forty-fourth year of the Ming imperial calendar (1616), Nurhaci turned against Ming and founded the Jin dynasty, which was later called the Later Jin. He defeated the Ming army in the Battle of

Sarhū two years later. He occupied Shenyang, a strategic town of Ming, and made it the capital. His son Hong Taiji changed the name of the dynasty from Later Jin to Qing in April 1636, as well as that of his people from Jurchen to Manchu in 1635.

In May 1644, Qing regent Dorgon responded to the appeal of Wu Sangui, former Ming general guarding the Shanhai Pass, rooted out Chinese rebel leader Li Zicheng. Given an opportunity that was too good to be missed, the Manchus entered the Central Plain and chose Beijing as the capital. In October 1911 (the year of the Xinhai), the eruption of the Wuchang Uprising led to the abdication of the Xuantong Emperor, bringing an end to the rule of over two hundred and sixty years of the Qing dynasty.

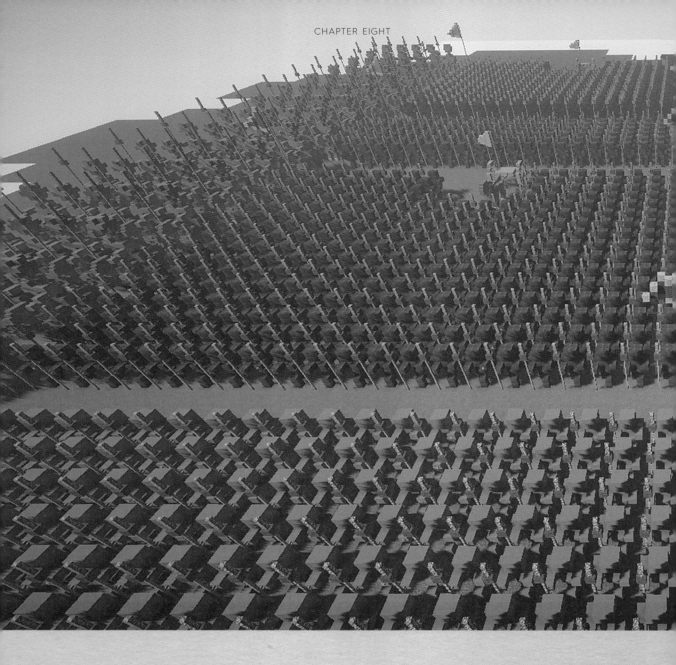

The Qing dynasty ruled by the Manchus formed a formidable military alliance with the Mongols. The Manchus conquered the Central Plain and demanded the subordination of Han Chinese. Beijing, where the Manchus called home, was divided into eight sectors, each of which was assigned to one of the Eight Banners. Manchu garrison camps were set up in the downtown of important cities. The bannermen and their families stationed and resided in Xi'an, Nanjing, Hangzhou, Fuzhou, Guangzhou, Chengdu, Jingzhou and more than ten other cities, which gradually became the Manchus in different parts of China now. Membership in the Eight Banners was hereditary and bannermen were granted land and income. The banners began to fall behind and lost their martial spirit as well as fighting capabilities over a century of relatively peaceful times. They collapsed at the first sign of resistance during the reigns of the Jiaqing Emperor and Daoguang Emperor.

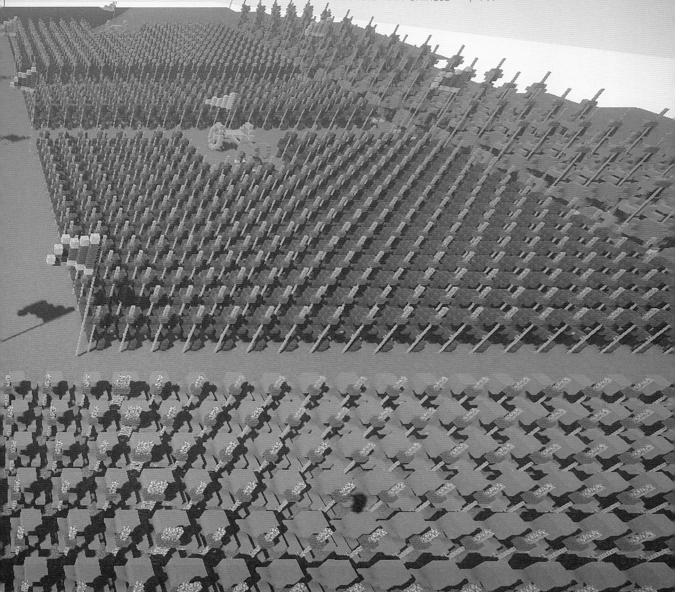

TOOLKIT

1
Stone

4
Cobblestone

67
Cobblestone
Stairs

109
Stone
Brick Stairs

35:4
Yellow Wool

35:11
Blue Wool

35:13
Green Wool

35:14
Red Wool

ARCHITECTURE

The Mukden Palace has houses with low ceilings and rooms with bed stoves. The Hall of Great Affairs located in the east of the palace was the venue for the military parade of the Qing emperor. In front of the octagonal hall was a huge square with eight pavilions for the leaders of the Eight Banners.

TOP

HALL OF GREAT AFFAIRS
(HALL FOR MILITARY DISCUSSIONS)

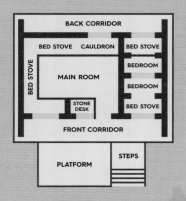

QINGNING PALACE
(LIVING QUARTERS OF THE EMPEROR AND HIS CONSORTS)

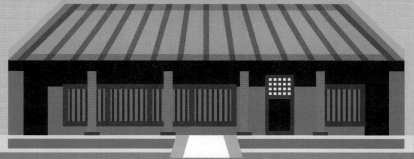

In the Qing capital Beijing, the Forbidden City where the emperor lived and the Western Park (now Zhongnanhai) right next to it demonstrates architectural style of Han. The hall of red walls and yellow tiles has a symmetrical structure along the axis in the middle. The colourful paintings and other interior decorations, however, demonstrate rich Manchu aesthetics. The plaque on the door is written in both Manchu and Han Chinese. Many landscape gardens with Jiangnan touch can still be found in Beijing and Chengde. The Summer Palace reconstructed by Empress Dowager Cixi is a complex that marks the integration of Han and Tibetan arts.

I   **I**   **Interior multi-coat decorative painting at the Qingning Palace, Shenyang**

II   **II**   **Glazed decorative painting at the South Loft Pavilion of the Hall of Supreme Harmony**

III   **III**   **The front and back hall (Han style at the front and east Tibetan style at the back) of the summer resort Pule Temple**

THE WANLI EMPEROR OF MING

THE QIANLONG EMPEROR OF QING

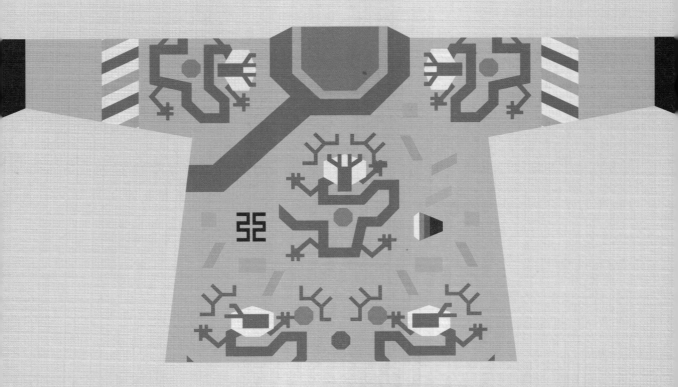

ATTIRE OF THE QING EMPEROR

**EMPRESS XIAODUANXIAN OF
THE WANLI EMPEROR**

**EMPRESS XIAOHUIZHANG OF
THE SHUNZHI EMPEROR OF QING**

 # ATTIRE

Manchu clothes were rather different from that of Han Chinese. Han Chinese wore loose-fitting robes and scholars put on square scarves. Manchus wore high-collar, slimming-sleeves dresses with magua jackets. Men shaved the front of their heads and combed the remaining hair into the queue hairstyle. For headwear, commoners wore pointed hats; the nobles and high-ranking officials used various pearls; military officers attached a peacock feather to the top of their cap. During the Qing dynasty, Han Chinese were forced to wear only Machu clothes and men were required to shave their hair to prove their loyalty and submission. As the popular saying of the hair-cutting order went, "Keeping the hair loses the head; cutting the hair keeps the head." On the other hand, the Qing adopted the tradition of Han Chinese and embroidered dragons on the left and right sides of the Dragon Robe of the Qing emperor. The axe motif embroidered on the right side represented power and the black and white bows in mirroring positions signified the virtue of goodness over evil.

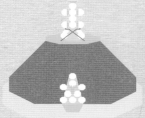

**CROWN OF THE
QING EMPEROR**

**DIADEM OF THE
QING EMPRESS**

皇建有極

I   **Calligraphy by Qianlong**

II   **Siku Quanshu**

III   **Kangxi Dictionary**

CULTURE AND LITERATURE

Upon its entrance into the Central Plain, the four Qing emperors – the Shunzhi Emperor, Kangxi Emperor, Yongzheng Emperor, and Qianlong Emperor – were committed to abolishing the malpractices (such as the political manipulation of eunuchs, negligence of the emperors, half-heartedness of officials) of the Ming dynasty and addressing social problems. They were also eager to learn the language and classics of Han Chinese to gain recognition from Han scholars. The triumphant conquests of various regional forces including Outer Mongolia, the Dzungar Khanate, Qinghai, Tibet, the Uyghur region, and Taiwan made possible the grand unification as well as the "High Qing" era for more than a century. The Qing reign coloured the Central Plain with vibrant cultures of Manchu, Mongolia, Tibet, and Uyghur. While some Han Chinese found the hair-shaving order humiliating, the sinicizing initiatives of the Qing monarch enabled Han culture to thrive and flourish. Han scholars were appointed important positions in the court and the Han learning, cultures and arts were also promoted. Prominent examples of the Han canon include the compilation of the Kangxi Dictionary and Imperial Encyclopaedia ordered by the Kangxi Emperor and the Siku Quanshu commissioned by the Qianlong Emperor.

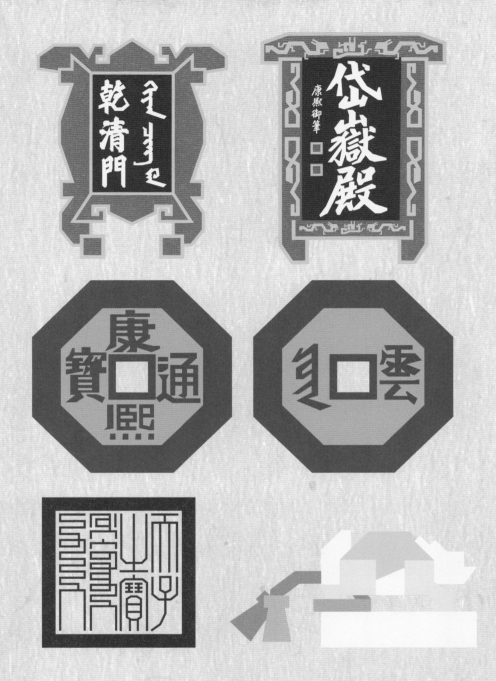

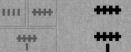

	Qianqing gate (Manchu and Han characters)
	Calligraphy by Kangxi
	Kangxi coin (Manchu and Han characters)
	"The Emperor's Treasure" (Manchu and Han characters)
	Imperial jade seal

MANCHU HAN IMPERIAL FEAST

CUISINE

The Manchu cuisine showcases the nomadic hunting and fishing of their ancestors. The Machus enjoy lamb and venison and drink honey and yoghurt on daily basis. Hotpot is a popular choice in winter. The world-renowned Manchu Han Imperial Feast is an interpretation of Han cooking and banqueting upon the group's entrance into the Central Plain.

BUN CAKE

KANGXI TRICOLOUR DISH SET, IDEAL FOR CONTAINING AND SHOWING DIFFERENT MEATS.

SACHIMA

TIN BOWL WITH GOLD-PLATED LONGEVITY CHARACTERS

TIN STOVE WITH LONGEVITY CHARACTERS

Minecraft X History 1 :

THE EIGHT WONDERS OF CHINA

by

**Cheung Wai Kwok,
Koding Kingdom & Ko Sing**

AUTHORS :   Cheung Wai Kwok (Text),
                  Koding Kingdom (Minecraft) &
                  Ko Sing (Illustration)

EDITOR :   Anne Lee
TRANSLATOR :   Yoyo Chan
ENGLISH EDITOR : Carrie Kwai
DESIGNER :   Die Leung

First published in November 2017
Published by Joint Publishing (H.K.) Co., Ltd.
20/F., North Point Industrial Building, 499 King's Road,
North Point, Hong Kong

Printed by Elegance Printing & Book Binding Co., Ltd.
Block A, 4/F, Hoi Bun Industrial Building, 6 Wing Yip Street, Kwun Tong,
Kowloon, Hong Kong

Distributed by SUP Publishing Logistics (H.K.) Ltd.
3/F., 36 Ting Lai Road, Tai Po, N.T., Hong Kong